LAGOS

TRAVEL

GUIDE

LAGOS

TRAVEL

GUIDE

FUNKE OGUNKOYA-FUTI

FIRST EDITION

Matador
9 Priory Business Park,
Wistow Road, Kibworth Beauchamp,
Leicestershire. LE8 0RX
Tel: 0116 279 2299
Email: books@troubador.co.uk
Web: www.troubador.co.uk/matador
Twitter: @matadorbooks

ISBN 978 1838593 100

British Library Cataloguing in Publication Data.
A catalogue record for this book is available from the British Library.

Typeset in 10pt Ten Oldstyle by Troubador Publishing Ltd, Leicester, UK

Matador is an imprint of Troubador Publishing Ltd

For my husband, Guy and my daughter, Fisayo.

CONTENTS

FOREWORD
BY MR SOLA OYINLOLA

My long career as a finance executive has offered me the
privilege of traversing continents. Having worked and lived in
multiple countries within Europe, Africa, Asia, the Middle East,
the UK, as well as the USA, I am a proponent of the truth that
our world has become smaller. As a people, we are no longer
restricted to time, space, or geographical location, and we have all
embraced globalisation through advancements in technology and
telecommunication.

Living beyond the borders of one nation exposes you to a
diverse range of cultures, people, languages, and experiences.
Without a doubt, there is no gainsaying the fact that every city
comes with its own perks; every city has its own edge. It has its
limitations, its strengths, and its secrets which are only known by
true indigenes.

As a Nigerian, I am testament to the amazing things you would
find in the nation, especially in the city of Lagos – the commercial
hub, bristling with industries and the technological capital of the
nation. In Lagos, there is so much to see and appreciate from the
sights, the sounds, and the wonders.

In order to be truly part of a city and enjoy what it stands for,
you are better off navigating it through the eyes of its inhabitants as
opposed to painstakingly going through the peculiarities of being a

stranger in unknown territories. For this, one would typically need a tour guide. However, if Lagos is the city you want to explore, this body of work would save you the stress and the cost of having a full-time tour guide.

The *Lagos Travel Guide* gives you a ringside ticket to where the best experiences lie. It takes you through the biggest neighbourhoods in Lagos, highlighting what makes them tick and what you stand to enjoy from them. Through pages exploring restaurants, your senses are heightened as you have a first-hand dive into the food culture of the city. It explores the resorts, the nightlife, arts and culture, and even the best places to stay when in Lagos. The interviews in this guide cut across a wide spectrum of Lagos dwellers from the affluent celebrities to the everyday men and women living various versions of their Lagos experience, thereby showing you the different voices of the city.

This amazing piece of work comes with little surprise for me. Written by someone who is an avid tourist and has travelled the world, engaging with a diverse range of cultures and societies, she no doubt has an eye for the best. While she does have an international exposure to what the tourist wants, she doubles as a true local herself, having spent most of her life in the city.

Funke has always been one to explore vastly and it is that same need for exploration that has led her to create this picturesque guide. As such, the book showcases both the high-end luxury lifestyle of the city together with its local perks. This piece isn't just for the foreigners as I too have not explored many of the sites unveiled here.

There is no doubt that tourism has gone beyond just a form of exploration, hospitality, or relaxation. Tourism is now a prime driver for many economies across the world, and Nigeria, starting from the city of Lagos, is set to become one of the most prominent ones in Africa. This guide serves as a catalyst for the development of the tourism industry in the nation, as it gives you a fresh, unbiased narrative which is the true picture of the city.

I must admit that it is a timely and well-researched work that is relevant to both Nigerians and foreigners alike. Lagos has so much to offer and as long as you are in the city, this book would serve as an asset you cannot do without.

INTRODUCTION

"This is African energy. The one I discovered here
in Lagos when I was 23. The one I am glad to see is
still thriving several years later. The one I hope many
Europeans will get to know. The one that is far from the
African prejudice of misery."

**– President of France,
Emmanuel Macron**

There are some places you never truly forget. The sounds, the
sights, the smells, and the feelings linger on long after you leave.
For some, it is because of the grandiosity of the high-rising, state-
of-the-art infrastructure. For others, it is because of the richness
of culture represented in the music and food. And still for others,
it is due to the breathtaking countryside, bustling market squares,
business districts, the people, and the memories shared.

In Lagos, it is all of those things together, along with the perfect
dose of drama, chaos, and mysticism. You never quite know Lagos
until you become a part of it, breathing its air of opportunities,
tasting its home-cooked meals, dancing to the music of its
heartbeat, laughing with its people.

As a non-Lagosian, all of this awesomeness (and drama) can
give you the most amazing experience. However, it can also be

chaotic – especially when you're detached from the system. This guide will help you as a visitor be a part of the beauty that is Lagos, while also navigating the chaos that it can be. Not only does this guide help save you from the darker parts of the city, it exposes you to the culture that is rooted in respect and gives you a first-class ride to where the magic actually happens.

In this guide, some local legends tell their Lagos story. I speak with a world-famous art and culture icon, a Nollywood actor, a tricycle rider, an inspiring media personality, and a famous chef. A feature showcases "Made in Nigeria", highlighting notable fashion designers, must-read books, must-watch films, and the local music worth digging into. Get immersed in the sights, sounds, and flavours of the city. Get immersed in Lagos.

KEY

ACCOMMODATION

ARTS

BEACH

CULTURE

FOOD

HISTORICAL

LITERATURE

MONUMENT

NIGHTLIFE

OUTDOORS

RESORT

SHOPPING

Victoria Island is an affluent neighbourhood in Lagos and the central hub for large corporations – call it the Wall Street of Lagos. It is also home to many expatriates and employees of multinational companies as well as the location for many diplomatic offices. Here you will find the US Embassy, British Deputy High Commission, and the Deputy High Commission of Canada amongst many other consulates and embassies. Victoria Island has evolved over the years to be a place of choice to live, work, and play.

VICTORIA ISLAND

Yellow Chilli Restaurant & Bar

If you're looking for somewhere with an amazing ambience and great food, then Yellow Chilli is a great place to start. Their signature Seafood Okra is a talk of the town and something you should definitely try if you're visiting for the first time. Try it with some other dishes like eba (cassava starch) or boiled plantain. Yellow Chilli is a safe bet for traditional Nigerian meals in Victoria Island if you do not want to venture into street food. In Victoria Island Yellow Chilli is located at *27 Oju Olobun Close, Victoria Island,* and there is also a branch located at *35 Joel Ogunaike Street, Ikeja.*

Yellow Chilli

Eko Hotel & Suites

Eko Hotel & Suites

One of the most prominent hotels in Lagos, Eko Hotel takes pride in its luxurious ambience. The property is a five-star hotel and is acclaimed as the most preferred hotel in West Africa. Guests have unbridled access to the Atlantic Ocean, gym facilities, spa and sauna, laundry services, eight amazing restaurants, seven bars, a world-class swimming pool, and more than 800 well-furnished rooms. It provides the ultimate luxurious escape and shields you from all the noise of the outside. Eko Hotel & Suites is located at *Plot 1415 Adetokunbo Ademola Street, Victoria Island.*

Eko Hotel Arts & Crafts Market

Eko Hotel Arts & Crafts Market

Nestled in the grounds of the famous Eko Hotel & Suites is this arts and crafts market. The market is also the base for money traders, popular with tourists looking to change their foreign currency – the foreign exchange rate given here tends to be favourable. Make sure to visit this well-organised market if you are looking for art pieces, from brass work to jewellery, to furnish your home with or bring back as gifts. Take your time to navigate this market and use your bargaining skills to negotiate a great price – if you can, visit with a local to get the best deal. The market is open daily and is located at *Plot 1415 Adetokunbo Ademola Street, Victoria Island.*

Terra Kulture 🛍 🍴 🏛

One of the most popular literary and arts centres, Terra Kulture is located in the heart of Victoria Island. This is a great place to start if you want a taste of the theatre and arts in Lagos. Before your performance, head next door to the Terra Kulture restaurant where you can try palm wine in a traditional calabash or indulge in a traditional Nigerian meal. Terra Kulture is the brain child of Bolanle Austin-Peters, a Nigerian lawyer and businesswoman, who founded this educational and recreational organisation in 2003 to promote the richness and diversity of Nigerian languages, arts, and culture. The venue also boasts a mini gallery and a souvenir shop.

Terra Kulture is located at 1376 Tiamiyu Savage Street, Victoria Island.

Terra Kulture

Lagos Oriental Hotel

Lagos Oriental Hotel 🏨

Off the popular Ozumba Mbadiwe Road in Victoria Island, the rooms at the Lagos Oriental Hotel have enchanting views of the Lagos lagoon. The rooms at the hotel offer guests a unique combination of luxury and style, ranging in size from 60 to 300 square metres. Where modern style meets unquestionable comfort, Lagos Oriental Hotel's guestrooms also feature original artwork that complement the Asian furnishings. The muted colour schemes contrast with a backdrop of city lights and skyscrapers. All rooms have LCD flat-screen televisions, wired or wireless internet access, individual air-conditioning control, in-room safe, complimentary tea and coffee-making facilities, and luxurious bathrobes and slippers. The Lagos Oriental Hotel is also known for its top-class banquet and meeting facilities. Lagos Oriental Hotel is located at *3 Lekki Road, Victoria Island.*

Tarkwa Bay

If you're looking for a perfect place to relax on a weekend, away from the hustle and bustle of working and living on the island, then board a high-speed boat to this sheltered beach near Lagos Harbour. The boat ride takes about 15 minutes from Victoria Island to the beach and if you're looking to have a weekend getaway, the beach also has beach houses that can be rented for a weekend getaway. Unlike other beaches in Lagos that can get really busy, Tarkwa Bay isn't often noisy or overcrowded, especially during the week. Board a boat to this island from Fiki Marina which is located at *3/4 Ozumba Mbadiwe Avenue, Victoria Island.*

Tarkwa Bay

Art Café 🍴 🏛

Step into Lagos' most artsy café. If you can imagine what a café/restaurant with an outside terrace lodged upon its own gallery looks like, then you would have imagined Art Café. This is where expats and creatives alike meet to work, relax, and indulge in a bite or two. The décor of the café is infused with Nigerian art, right down to the furniture. Even more amazing is that the artwork inside the café is changed every two weeks to promote the gallery on the floor below. It is key to note that most of the furniture within the café (from the lamp shades to the tables) can be purchased. Art Café is located at *282 Akin Olugbade Street, Victoria Island.*

Art Café

Maison Fahrenheit Hotel

Maison Fahrenheit Hotel

Maison Fahrenheit is an urban oasis minutes away from popular clubs, high-profile business organisations, art galleries, parks, and the Atlantic Ocean. Here, urban energy collides with a glamorous, fantasy-satisfying escape. Maison Fahrenheit celebrates the Nigerian modern zeitgeist and connects that to the rest of the world. With iconic designs and contemporary luxury, the boutique hotel accommodates different needs gracefully. One of the best things about Maison Fahrenheit is that it's artsy. It makes use of crafts and fine art in a perfect blend of simplicity and ornamentation to create attractive aesthetics. The property is located at *80 Adetokunbo Ademola Street, Victoria Island.*

Mega Plaza

Mega Plaza

If you're looking for a place to purchase a myriad of things, from food to home appliances to gift boxes, then Mega Plaza will meet your needs. An ultra-modern, five-floor shopping mall with more than 60 stores and restaurants, Mega Plaza is one of the first malls constructed in Lagos. It is known as the go-to mall in the area for electronics as well as food, as it also hosts a number of restaurants. Mega Plaza is located at *14 Idowu Martins Street, Victoria Island*.

Mama Zi 👜

Are you looking for a unique artisanal range of products that are locally designed, sourced, and inspired? Mama Zi is where you need to be. You'll find unique products to use and take home as gifts for those who want to wear a piece of Nigeria with them. Mama Zi is located at *4a Akin Olugbade, Victoria Island.*

Pizza-Riah 🍴

Pizza-Riah is probably the most popular pizza spot on the Victoria Island axis. If you're looking for great thin-crust pizza with amazing toppings, you'll love it here. Straight out of the books of Italians, the pizza here is made in a traditional wood-fired oven, which gives the pizza a very authentic taste. They also serve chicken and meat suya (spicy meat) – a must-try. The restaurant has both outdoor and indoor seating and is very laid-back with great prices as well. Pizza-Riah is located at *13 Musa Yar' Adua Street, Victoria Island.*

Pizza-Riah

XO Boutique Bakery

XO Boutique Bakery

The brain-child of Chef Alex, a Nigerian–Russian chef who trained at the Pacific Institute of Culinary Arts (PICA) in Vancouver, Canada, XO Boutique Bakery features traditional French and new-world breads and pastries with a modern flair. XO Boutique Bakery is located at *48 Balarabe Musa Crescent, Victoria Island*.

La Taverna

La Taverna

Another amazing pizza spot located in Victoria Island, La Taverna is acclaimed by many as having the best pizza in Lagos. Known for its popular wine and pizza meal deals on select weekdays, this warm and cosy restaurant is the creation of Cristian Duhalde Diaz, a Chilean chef. The restaurant is popular amongst the expat community in the area and it shares the same compound with XO Bakery. La Taverna is located within a hotel called Palais Royal, at _48 Balarabe Musa Crescent, Victoria Island._

Craft Gourmet by Lou Baker 🍴

Craft Gourmet is a French restaurant located on the last floor of Mega Plaza, an iconic mall on Victoria Island. Craft Gourmet is where to spot the who's who of Lagos, especially on weekends – it's quite popular with the expatriate community in Lagos. The décor of Craft Gourmet really stands out, which means the restaurant rarely does much to market its establishment. Even though the restaurant has a French style of cooking, its menu incorporates West African dishes. Craft Gourmet is located at *14 Idowu Martins Street, Victoria Island.*

Craft Gourmet

Vellvett Grill & Lounge 🍸 🍴

Set in a quiet street in Victoria Island, Vellvett is the go-to nightlife spot for those living on the Ikoyi-Victoria Island axis. Vellvett Grill & Lounge is part of the Blowfish Group, which is based in Lagos. The restaurant serves a mix of international, grill, and Asian cuisines, with a variety of meals offered in a standard lounge setting. It's very popular on Fridays and Saturdays amongst the cool kids of Lagos, so make sure to book a table ahead of time as it can get very cramped otherwise. If you're looking for Afrobeat or a classical ambience, Vellvett is the place to be. Vellvett Grill & Lounge is located at *19B Idejo Street, Victoria Island.*

Vellvett Grill & Lounge

The Homestores

The Homestores 🛍 🎭

Within the same vicinity of Art Café is The Homestores. The Homestores is a tourist haven for fans of arts and culture who will be spoilt for choice from clay works and incense, to candles and Terra works. Whether you are looking to build your home art collection or simply seeking to buy African goods for family and friends, this is where to go. The Homestores is located at *282 Akin Olugbade Street, Victoria Island.*

Zenbah

Zenbah 🍸

Zenbah is one of the most stunning bars in Lagos. Perfect for after-work hangouts with friends, guests enjoy exceptional cocktails with an aura of class and fun. The drinks menu is one to be envied. They serve an impressive and extensive menu of world-renowned contemporary cocktails made by some of the finest local and international bartenders. This nightlife venue is very popular with the residents of Victoria Island and entry here can be tricky given its demand. It's a popular Thursday-night spot within Lagos so make sure to get there early. Zenbah is located at *11B Akin Adesola Street, Victoria Island.*

Nok By Alara 🍴🏛️

Ambience, ambience, ambience. Nok By Alara is the brain-child of Reni Folayiwo. Alara offers the utmost luxurious fashion for Nigerians while also producing custom-made, authentic African furniture. Nok By Alara is an ethno-fusion restaurant that gives a nostalgic feel of vintage West Africa. The restaurant takes African staples in a different direction and amazing cocktails are also on the menu. Nok By Alara is a popular spot for business meetings during the day and after-work drinks. The building houses both an exhibition-style retail space for Alara Stores as well as the restaurant. Nok By Alara is located at *12a Akin Olugbade Street, Victoria Island.*

Nok By Alara

Hard Rock Café 🍴 🍸

If you want to have a taste of the beautiful entertainment hub that is Lagos, then a visit to Hard Rock Café is a must. Located on the beach of Victoria Island, Hard Rock Café is a rock 'n' roll-themed chain with a high-energy vibe, serving burgers and American classics. Since launching in 2016, it has hosted some of the coolest parties in Lagos and been frequented by celebrities, popular musicians, and DJs. It's also the set of some amazing contemporary music videos and the venue is famous for hosting many concerts in Lagos. It's a favourite for Lagosians as far as nightlife is concerned. Their classic menu consists of the American cuisine that makes Hard Rock Cafés famous around the world whilst also lending a Nigerian twist to some menu items. Hard Rock Café is located at *3/4 Water Cooperation Road, Landmark Village, Oniru, Victoria Island.*

Hard Rock Café

Shiro

Shiro 🍴

Located in the same vicinity as Hard Rock Café, Shiro, meaning "castle" in Japanese, is where to find the finest Asian cuisine and fabulous cocktails. Its signature high ceilings and grand statues epitomise the essence of Shiro. With ample parking and a beautiful al fresco area that overlooks the beach (which in turn has private cabanas and its own bar), Shiro is the perfect spot for a chilled-out evening or sundowner. It's the perfect beach getaway, right in the heart of Victoria Island. Shiro is located at *3/4 Water Cooperation Road, Landmark Village, Oniru, Victoria Island.*

INTERVIEW

with

CHIEF NIKE
DAVIES-OKUNDAYE

(PRINCIPAL ARTIST & FOUNDER, NIKE ART GALLERY)

Founder of the largest art gallery in West Africa, Nike Art Gallery, Chief Nike Davies-Okundaye is an internationally acclaimed artist and designer who was born in 1951 in Ogidi-Ijumu, Kogi State, Nigeria. She is the founder and director of four art centres that offer free training to young artists in visual, musical, and performing arts. Nike is known around the world for promoting her designs through exhibitions and workshops in Nigeria, the United States, Belgium, Germany, Austria, Italy, and the United Kingdom.

Chief Nike Davies-Okundaye knows art – and the Nigerian art scene knows her too. She grew up in an environment where traditional weaving was still practised, even as the tradition in her native village of Ogidi in Western Nigeria began to die. Chief Nike's artistic skills were nurtured at a young age by her parents and great-grandmother who were musicians and craftspeople. She got her first breakthrough in 1972 when a US agency came to Nigeria to recruit African artists to teach indigenous African art in the US. She returned to Nigeria with new ideas and methods in which she could apply her art.

Nike was recruited by a US agency in Nigeria as part of a group of ten African artists, to teach indigenous African art in the US

When did you become an artist?

My parents were craftspeople and I started learning at the age of six. That is how they passed on their knowledge to me. The first education I received was from them.

How were you able to carve a niche for yourself in the Nigerian art world?

Well, it is a lot of struggle to carve a niche as a woman in the art world. The truth is that you need to work ten times harder than a man because society believes that the world of art belonged to men alone. When I joined the society, women were always doing a lot of craft but the work they were doing usually took more than three weeks to complete. That work is no longer craft but art.

Many of my people were craftspeople and my great-grandmother was the head of the craftswomen in the village. When I moved to Osogbo, I joined the male artists. All the artists were men, but their teachers were female – the likes of Susan Wenger and Georgina Beyer. They were both female but the men would always say that the husbands of these women were their teacher because they were men. But Susan Wenger's husband was always

correcting them, saying, "I am a photographer and writer, not an artist. It is my wife that is an artist." So yes, you have to work ten times more as a woman.

What is your favourite piece of art?

Well it has to be my works. Let's talk about textiles. *Eniyan ni aso me* – what is the closest things to your skin? The closest thing to your skin is your fabric. If you are a woman, your husband is the closest thing to your skin; however, before you wear your husband, you wear textiles which is why textiles are very important. You cannot go out naked. *Eniyan ni aso me*. My fabrics are people; they are closer to me, so the art of textile is very powerful.

What inspires you about Lagos?

Lagos is the city of excellence and prosperity. Everyone knows that anyone who comes to Lagos and can put in the hard work will make money. When I was in Osogbo, I wasn't seeing the results of my hard work. They told me that Lagos was too clumsy, but I was determined to make my own "AJE" (money).

If you are selling an ordinary toothpick and you know how

to target your customers, you will make money. When I was in Osogbo, I worked with more than 100 women and we were campaigning for people to buy our dresses. When I moved to Lagos, the customers were coming by themselves in abundance. When people are aware of your product's good quality, they will come to patronise you. So yes, Lagos is the city of opportunities.

What did you learn during that first international breakthrough in 1972?

Firstly, I learnt that art could actually be profitable. They asked us to bring some of our learnings, things that would benefit our people. They took us to many states and we visited many galleries and museums. My first gallery was my bedroom – a room shared with 15 wives and kids. I remember waking up in the morning, I would lay my mat and *adire* on the floor and I would beg the other wives to not let their kids create a mess on it. I had a chance to see how an actual gallery should look like, so that was one of the things I brought back to create my own gallery. Secondly, I also learnt that, in the US, most women had a man to themselves. I started a revolution back home and that's how all we wives left.

How would you describe the Lekki area, where your Lagos gallery is located?

Approximately ten years ago, many were afraid to even stop here in Lekki. Lekki, however, has become the heart and core of Lagos. We moved here in 1994 after spending two years building our house here. We like living here.

Where is your favourite part of Lagos to eat?

I like Lekki, but to be honest I cook my own food in the house. I love cooking.

How would you describe the art scene in Lagos?

The art scene in Lagos has grown thanks to the young generation who have made art more contemporary for people to display in their homes. In the past, only a very small amount of people were interested in art, but this has changed. The return of those in the diaspora has helped. Also, the many collectors and artists who studied overseas have helped the art scene as they created awareness for Nigerian art.

In the past we didn't consider photography as art; only painters and blacksmiths. Now I see more

Nigerians actually purchasing art. Also, without the writers, no one will know anything about art so that is why writing, and journalism, play a very important role in supporting art.

Are there any young artists that we should know about?

I will start from Rom Isichei and Chief Tola Wewe. These people have masters and MFAs in art. My son Isinayiwa is also a beader like me, a dancer, a carver, and a drummer. He is also into photography. Then to the younger artists: Badejo Abiodun, Akeem Adeleke, Asiko. There are a lot of them.

What is special about Lagos?

When we mention Lagos, we mention Nigeria. Home. It is the only place I don't need a visa for. When I travel, they often ask me to go and queue for a visa. When I come to my country, they just stamp my passport. There is something about Lagos even with her hustle and bustle. It is a city that never sleeps. If something is in New York today, it will be in Lagos tomorrow. Also, I love the club sandwich here even though it has cholesterol; the best club sandwich is the one in Lagos.

Where can we find the best club sandwich in Lagos?

At the Radisson Blu Ikeja (it used to be called Renaissance). It has the best club sandwich in Nigeria. Also at the Wheatbaker. When I have guests that want something other than African food, I take them to the Wheatbaker in Ikoyi, or Cactus in Victoria Island.

Where do you go to relax in Lagos?

I go to Oba Art Gallery & Suites where I can sleep in art. You wake up in art and you can relax in art. The place was built because of the King of Morocco. When the King of Morocco came to Nigeria, he wanted to sleep in my art gallery, but I said, "Your Excellency, but there is no bathroom here." So, I told myself that before he comes back to Nigeria, I will create a place that embodies art. The bed is art, the treasure boxes are art. You are completely surrounded by art.

Where is the most beautiful and intriguing part of Lagos?

The Governor's place in Alausa, Maryland. When you visit some parts of Maryland and Ikeja, you forget you are in a city filled with traffic. Back in the days when

Lagbaja used to play there, it was full of life and bubbly. I love Lagbaja.

What are the top three galleries you would recommend for a visitor to Lagos?

Of course I will mention my own Nike Art Gallery here in Lekki. Terra Kulture is another great one by Bolanle Austin-Peters in Victoria Island, and finally, Signature Beyond Art Gallery in Ikoyi. All three galleries are run by women. There are about 45 galleries in Nigeria, although many are run by foreigners. But no one can run our galleries like us.

What does a typical day in your life look like, for instance, on a Monday?

I don't like to give out money on Monday. I like to receive money so when people come with their money problems, I say, "You should have come around yesterday." I like to spend Monday receiving money but if you spend the day spending money, you will spend all your money and millions throughout the week. Fela has a song about spending money. He says, "Don't give me bad luck on Monday."

What do you think is the biggest challenge when it comes to tourism in Nigeria to Lagos?

It is the visas. Visas need to be made available for tourists on arrival. Some people currently travel over 600 kilometres in their country to apply at the Nigerian embassy, so that they can then spend their money. Security is also very important. But before security, they need to look at the visa issue which is something the government is working on.

"If life dey

show you pepper,

my guy make

pepper soup."

PIDGIN PROVERB

Arguably the most affluent neighbourhood in Lagos, Ikoyi is much more residential than neighbouring Victoria Island. It's known as the choice of residence for upper-class Nigerians and it's also known for its social club Ikoyi Club 1938, a members-only club where the elite of Lagos mingle over a round of golf or a game of tennis. It's also home to Banana Island (an artificial island) and Parkview, which is home to a gated community where residents experience luxury services like 24-hour electricity and round-the-clock security. Only the billionaires of Africa, high net-worth celebrities, and the crème de la crème live here.

The George

The George 🏢

Since its debut in July 2015, independent luxury boutique hotel, The George has rapidly established a name for itself. It caters to the needs of the discerning business traveller looking for a unique and personalised hotel stay and those seeking the comfort, safety, tranquillity, and quality of a five-star hotel. The George boasts 60 individually appointed en-suite rooms, ranging from classic rooms to penthouse suites with fittings and facilities of exceptional quality. At The George, customer service is at its finest and the restaurant has a wide range of international and local dishes. The George is located at *No. 30 Lugard Avenue, Ikoyi.*

Casa Lydia Bistro 🍴

Set in a compound on Glover Road, this Italian restaurant is known by locals for its seafood pasta – a melody of prawns, calamari, and white fish. It is a contemporary and quaint resto/café that is co-located with La Provence within the quiet shores of Ikoyi. Their array of cocktails is impressive and you can also find local, traditional Nigerian dishes here. The menu is mainly Italian with continental influences ranging from American-style burgers to spicy seafood platters. Consistency is something this establishment is known for. Casa Lydia Bistro is located at *19 Glover Road, Ikoyi.*

Casa Lydia

Bogobiri House ♉ 🏛 🏢

Bogobiri House is known for its rich and unique array of entertainment and events, from its Thursday-night Freedom Hall to its Tuesday-night TARUWA. These events offer a platform for new talent in spoken word and music and Bogobiri also hosts weekend high life, jazz, and Afrobeat shows by more established performers. Bogobiri is a magnetic hub in which to eat, lounge, enjoy good music, and connect with people in a relaxed, chilled-out environment. Set within the Bogobiri House is a sixteen-room boutique hotel. It is located at *9 Maitama Sule Street, off Awolowo Road, Ikoyi.*

Bogobiri

Ikoyi Club

Ikoyi Club 🌳 🍴

Ikoyi Club is where the big guys come to relax. It's a prestigious sports and relaxation club known to host the elites in Lagos. It was formally established as a European club in 1938 and has maintained its elite status all these years, making it an ideal place for developing business relationships. The club occupies 456 acres of land, giving it ample space for its golf course, tennis courts, badminton courts, and squash platform. If you're hungry after all that activity, the chicken and beef suya served at Ikoyi Club has a great reputation. Entry is via membership only but members can bring in guests for a fee. Ikoyi Club is located at *6 Ikoyi Club 1938 Road, Ikoyi.*

Samantha's Bistro

Samantha's Bistro

Even though it's popular amongst Ikoyi inhabitants for its burgers and smoothies, Samantha's Bistro also serves French, Nigerian, and Italian cuisine. This well-known restaurant is located on a very quiet road in Ikoyi and it's popular with the expat community in Lagos for lunch and dinner meetings. Make sure to try their burger the first time you visit. Samantha's Bistro is located at *No 2 Olawale Daodu Road, Ikoyi.*

Glover Court Suya

Glover Court is probably the most popular joint for suya in the Victoria Island/Ikoyi area. They even call themselves, "The Suya Capital of Lagos". Whether it's beef suya, kidney suya, liver suya, or chicken suya, they have it all. Expect a long queue if you're visiting late in the evenings but the wait is worth it. There is no in-dining here and all food is wrapped up in newspaper cuttings, just as all authentic suya in Lagos is. If you don't like spicy food, be sure to tell them to ease up on the suya pepper. Glover Court Suya is located at *37 Glover Court, off Glover Road, Ikoyi.*

Glover Court

Jazzhole 🎭 📚 🏛️

If you like the idea of books, coffee, tea, pastries, and amazing music, this place is the ultimate destination for you. Located on one of the busiest roads on the island and recommended by award-winning Nigerian author Chimamanda Ngozi Adichie, Jazzhole takes you into an oasis away from the hustle outside. Visit Jazzhole to buy classic music, read, and if you're lucky, catch a jazz evening with an up-and-coming artist. It's also the perfect place to grab a coffee and cake whilst being surrounded by history and music. Jazzhole is located at *168 Awolowo Road, Ikoyi.*

Jazzhole

Quintessence

Quintessence

Established in 1967 by Swedish–Nigerian Chief Mrs Aino Oni-Okpaku, Quintessence has been running to promote and develop arts and crafts for local Nigerian content. Expect to find a huge range of authentic arts, crafts, textiles, and furnishings. More recently, Quintessence has organised exhibitions and fashion shows on-site to offer visual artists opportunities to promote their works. If you're looking for authentic gifts from Nigerian books and music, to art to take back home, Quintessence is the shop to visit. Quintessence is located at *Parkview Estate by the entrance, off Gerrard Road, Ikoyi.*

INTERVIEW
with
SAMUEL OGUNDARE
(CORPORATE KEKE DRIVER)

Samuel Ogundare is a 30-year-old tricycle rider who is passionate about changing the service culture in Nigeria by serving Nigerians in a professional and corporate manner. He is the creator of the Corporate Keke brand in Nigeria. Born in Ile-Ife, Osun state (a state north-east of Lagos), Samuel is a professional who loves family and music. He moved to Lagos from Ile-Ife in 2013 in search of opportunity and prosperity. His desire to improve the service of an everyday product that millions of Lagosians use every day has put him on the map. He shares with us his vision for the state of transportation in the city and how Lagos and Lagosians have changed his life for the better.

What led you to moving to Lagos?

After completing my secondary school studies, I had no funds to go to university. My father is retired but used to work in agriculture and my mum is a businesswoman. I have four siblings so things were financially difficult. My older brother (based in Lagos) convinced me to move here in 2013. When I arrived, I decided to become a tricycle rider and I have been doing that ever since. I started out driving on a hire purchase agreement but I now own my own vehicle. God has been faithful to me.

When did you decide to change the way you dress?

It was about four years ago, in 2015. I simply wanted to do things in a different manner. I did not like the way tricycle drivers dressed and thought there must be a better way to serve my customers. So I changed the way I dressed and also invested in upgrading my Keke Napep (tricycle). I brought in a music system, a television, a fan, and changed the interior, amongst many other things, all to improve my customers' experience.

What has been the response from Lagosians?

Monetary-wise, my clients have been generous to me, more generous than when I wasn't delivering my corporate service. I would say four out of every five customers will pay me more than the standard price. They like the fact that I am professional and that I take my job seriously. They appreciate the concept but have been quite confused about my dressing on occasions, asking questions such as whether the Lagos heat makes me uncomfortable. They are sometimes surprised to hear that I am happy with my job. Outside of my job, vendors give me freebies because they are impressed with my appearance and mannerisms.

I have been featured on the biggest media platforms in Nigeria and the feedback has been nothing but encouraging. Many of the Nollywood movie stars have reached out to show their support for me and what I am trying to achieve. Overall, the support from my fellow Nigerians has been great. My family has also been very supportive and encouraging.

How have other Keke Napep drivers acted towards you?

Many enquire and ask how they can also become like me. I explain to them that it is not easy. That they need to invest in their clothes, equipment, etc. The clothes are not cheap. But I tell them that I am ready to put them through when they are indeed ready. I also explain to them that it goes beyond the clothes they wear. It is the whole experience they have to change, from how they speak to consumers, to attending to customers' needs during the journey.

What is your vision for this job?

I want tricycle riders to be seen as corporate workers. Just the same way personal drivers are perceived and how Uber drivers are seen. I want the jobs to be conducted by university graduates. There are many unemployed graduates who could do this job. I want it to be a job that people are proud of. I believe the experience for those living in Lagos and visiting Lagos would be greater. It would really set us apart as a city.

Where in Lagos do you live?

I live in an area called Surulere on the Lagos mainland. Surulere is a very lively area in Lagos with many cocktail bars, clubs, beer parlours, shopping malls, boutique shops, and banks. I like it here even though I am not a very social person. It is very good for my transportation business as there are many customers so I

tend to only work in this area. I would say this is my favourite part of Lagos.

What do you do for fun in Lagos?

I tend to only work Mondays to Fridays as I see myself as a corporate worker. I am an instrumentalist who plays the drums so my weekends tend to be me playing at rehearsals and visiting the Leisure Mall in Surulere. My Sundays are for church, for worshiping God, and also playing drums at church as I am part of the church band.

What is your favourite Nigerian meal and where do you go for it?

I love rice and plantain. My favourite restaurant is a local Buka in Surulere called Titi's Kitchen. It is located on 55 Abayomi Street. I go there with my cooler and tend to eat in my Keke Napep on a quiet street off the popular Bode Thomas Street in Surulere.

What do you love most about Lagos?

Lagos is a place where opportunities are available. I always tell people, "If you come to Lagos, you can pick money, especially if you are prepared to work hard." So yes, the opportunities are here.

What does a typical day look like for you in Lagos?

I wake up by 5 a.m., get ready, and clean my Keke Napep for the day. By 7 a.m., I head out to do a daily school charter run for my client. By 8 a.m., I am ready to start work. At 12 p.m., I find somewhere to park, turn on my fan, and relax for 30 minutes. At 12:30 p.m. I head back to work until 2 p.m. when I grab lunch from my favourite Buka. I try to finish work by 6 p.m. but extend to 7 p.m. if work is very busy. After that, I go home to rest.

What would you change about Lagos?

I would employ more graduates in government organisations like the police force. I believe appearance matters and would enforce government workers to portray themselves in a way that is more corporate and approachable.

"Today's newspaper na tomorrow Suya wrap."

PIDGIN PROVERB

Lekki is arguably the most up-and-coming area in Lagos state. This area, which was once a shanty town, has now evolved into a community that is envied by many. The Lekki Peninsula adjoins the commercial Victoria Island and the residential Ikoyi area. The area is not only home to many affluent residential estates but also to an accompanying commercial district that allows the area to function sufficiently by itself. Lekki is also home to many tourist point of interests, from the famous Nike Art Gallery to the Lekki Conservation Centre, which is home to the longest canopy walkway in Africa.

LEKKI

Lekki Art & Craft Market

Known to locals as Jakande Market, this hidden gem in Lekki is popular with locals and tourists. The organised market is a haven for artefacts. The market has different shops, which all have different artworks for sale, each piece coming from a different part of Nigeria. From paintings to wooden sculptures, to masks, to necklaces and bracelets, to woven bags and even crocodile bags, you can find it all here. This is the perfect spot to find those unique pieces to take back home or to give as gifts to friends and family. One tip is to be ready to barter at all times. Lekki Art & Craft Market is located at *Oba Elegushi Street, Off Lekki-Epe Expressway, Lekki.*

Lekki Art & Craft

La Campagne

La Campagne Tropicana Beach Resort

Looking to step away from the hustle and bustle of Lagos? This beach resort provides relaxation and more. Arguably the most exotic beach resort in Lagos, this four-star resort is located on the outskirts of Lekki and makes for a perfect day trip or weekend stay. You get to be part of the serenity and freshness of nature, watching trees sway as you bask in the beauty of the romantic reflection of the sun on the Atlantic Ocean. The beach here is well taken care of and there are many activities that will keep you busy, from volleyball to kayaking to horseback riding. It also has different cabanas, each with various price points and facilities to meet varying needs. A true home away from home, La Campagne Tropicana Beach Resort is located in *Ikegun, Ibeju-Lekki Area, Off Lekki/Epe Expressway.*

Nike Art Gallery

Nike Art Gallery

One of the easiest ways to describe Nike Art Gallery is to call it art heaven! This gallery exhibits and sells an array of Nigerian art, from traditional African paintings and sculptures to contemporary pieces. The gallery is three storeys high and will take you out of the hustle and bustle of Lagos and fill you with instant joy. Found within the three levels of this gallery are pieces from different tribes, cultures, religions, and classes. It also features art created by the founder herself, Chief Nike Okundaye. If you're lucky, you will get a chance to meet her, dressed in traditional attire, as she always is, and possibly take a picture or two. The gallery is located at *No. 2, Elegushi Road, Lekki.*

Lekki Conservation Centre

Lekki Conservation Centre is an outdoor forest covering 190 acres. Popular with the locals during the weekend, the centre is known for its 401-metre-long canopy walkway, which is reputed to be the longest canopy walkway in Africa. The two-kilometre boardwalk offers excellent nature walks and bird watching opportunities. You can also relax in its cabals with friends, play some of its amazing board games, climb and sit in the treehouse, to mention a few fun things. There are a number of animals you might see as well – look out for the friendly monkeys. Lekki Conservation Centre is located at *Km, 19 Lekki-Epe Expressway, Lekki.*

Lekki Conservation

Lekki-Ikoyi Link Bridge 🌿

If you're looking for a place to run outside during the cool mornings or evenings in Lagos, then the Lekki-Ikoyi Link Bridge is a great option. The bridge connects Lekki with the affluent area of Ikoyi. This bridge has become iconic in Lagos and is featured in many media outlets as a representation of the beauty and sophistication of Lagos. This cable-stayed bridge is 1.36 kilometres long and beautifully illuminated at night, which is the perfect time for a nightlife photo. The bridge was commissioned and opened to the public in 2013 by then governor of Lagos State, Babatunde Raji Fashola. It is located *between Lekki Phase 1 and Ikoyi.*

Lekki-Ikoyi Bridge

The Palms Shopping Mall

The Palms Shopping Mall

One of the first malls in Lagos, the Palms Mall is home to a cinema, a supermarket, many fast-food outlets, and a few stores selling things ranging from clothing to electrical items. If you're looking for your weekly grocery shop or home appliances, or even looking to go to see a movie, the Palms Mall is the place. It is conveniently positioned if you are based in Victoria Island or Lekki Phase 1. The Palms Shopping Mall is located on *1 Bisway Street, Maroko, Lekki.*

The View Rooftop

The View Rooftop

The view from this rooftop is arguably of one the best views of the ocean from Lekki. Opened in 2018, The View Rooftop sits atop five floors of Twin Waters. You have a view of the sky and sunset – all the elements for a romantic date. It offers the perfect serene experience away from the hustle and bustle of urban Lagos. Please note that ripped or torn clothing, active sportswear, and rubber sandals are not permitted. Enjoy the ocean view with a delicious cocktail and finger bites. The View Rooftop is located off *Remi Olowude Road, Lekki.*

788 on the Sea 🍴

Looking for a great seafood restaurant in Lagos? 788 on the Sea is your best answer – albeit an expensive one. This fine-dining restaurant opened in 2018 in the Twin Waters building. If you're a seafood lover, order the mixed seafood platter, which comes with lobster, crab, prawns, and calamari. The restaurant is also a great after-work spot. Have a go at their mouth-watering dishes with modern Italian inspirations or simply enjoy a glass of wine from their exquisite collection while you enjoy the view of the Atlantic from their outdoor terrace. 788 on the Sea is located on the *2nd Floor of Twin Waters, off Remi Olowude, Okunde Bluewater Zone, Lekki Phase 1.*

788 on the Sea

Farm City 🍴 🍸

Famous for its grilled fish, Farm City is one of the most popular restaurants in Lekki. It's located on the most notable street in Lekki, Admiralty Way. The restaurant overlooks the lagoon, which is a great spot for watching fancy speedboats whizz by along the skyline, as the Lekki-Ikoyi Link Bridge lights up the night. Make sure to order the grilled fish but be prepared for it to be spicy! The venue doubles as a nightlife spot and is popular on weekends. Farm City is located at *15 Admiralty Way, Lekki Phase 1, Lekki.*

Farm City

INTERVIEW
with
ALEX OKE

HEAD CHEF & FOUNDER, XO BOUTIQUE BAKERY

Lagos-based chef Alex Oke is passionate about bread, pastry, and confections. He trained in classical/ contemporary French cuisine at the Pacific Institute of Culinary Arts (PICA) in Vancouver, Canada, and also worked at Lear Faye in East Vancouver before returning to Nigeria. He is the owner of XO Boutique Bakery and an instructor at the Culinary Academy in Lagos.

Born in Ibadan, Oyo state (north-east of Lagos), Alex Oke is a perfectionist, workaholic, and lover of life and family. He shares with us his passion for food in Lagos, recommendations for great food destinations in the city, and also how he unwinds from the hustle and bustle of the city.

You studied to become a chef abroad. What led you back to Nigeria?

The opportunity to make a name for myself, and I was tired of being treated as someone that Western society had to tolerate. I want to be celebrated; I deserve it.

What inspired you to create XO Bakery?

Over the years, whilst training and perfecting my craft, I also envisioned that I would have my own French-style patisserie in Nigeria. My dream was to create something cosy and intimate and I guess the stars aligned for me and XO Bakery was born.

What do you like most and least about Lagos?

Lagos is an interesting place to live and work. I love the pace of Lagos. The pace is quite fast like many metropolitan cities in the world. Experiencing the high highs and the low lows on the same day makes the city quite fascinating. It is addictive for any adrenaline junkies – which most chefs are. So if you like fast-paced environments, you will love Lagos.

How would you like it to change?

A stronger dining culture driven by higher disposable incomes.

What is your home area like?

I live in Victoria Island, which is considered an affluent neighbourhood in the city of Lagos. I would describe my neck of the woods as calm. I think it is probably the only place on the island where you can still find lots of greenery. I love it!

Where do you like to eat?

I love to eat at a number of places. My favourite would have to be at the lunch and supper clubs hosted by Chef Benedict at La Taverna here in Victoria Island. Great dishes and good vibes every single time. I also like to visit local joints and, in particular, I am a fan of beef suya. I go to Glover Court in Ikoyi to get my dose of suya.

What is the Lagos food scene like now?

Thriving. Diverse. Innovative.

Are there any other restaurants you would recommend visiting?

Yes, certainly. I would suggest Tarragon in Ikoyi for the fine-dining experience. Definitely venture to RSVP for the vibes. They are very popular with residents of Victoria Island. But I would also say don't always be a traditionalist, look for a food pop-up event. Those are always the best way to mingle with the foodie scene.

If you had a day off in Lagos, how would you spend it, from morning to evening?

I would take a banana boat to Tarkwa Bay and stay there all day.

Now let's talk about Nigeria's famous cuisines. What is your favourite traditional dish?

It is definitely abula. Abula is a soup that is a combination of amala (yam flour), gbegiri, and ewedu. Gbegiri soup originates from the Yoruba tribe and is prepared with beans. Ewedu soup is a draw soup made from jute leaves. It is delicious.

Where in Lagos do you get this dish?

Any Buka (local "hole-in-the-wall" joint) but try the ones on the Lagos mainland. They are probably more authentic.

Where should we go for the famous jollof rice?

For jollof rice, go to Omo Jesus in Apapa on the Lagos mainland.

Where do you go to escape the hustle and bustle of the city?

To get away from the hustle, I go to the beach; it is my escape and it's the perfect escape. I usually go to Pop Beach Club on the weekends. It is a popular members' sports club located in Ilashe. It is located about a 30-minute boat ride from Victoria Island.

Lagos in a weekend: What would you recommend?

16/16. It is a gallery on Kofo Abayomi Street in Victoria Island. Venture to Terra Kulture to catch a stage play. Visit Alara, a concept store and restaurant, and hFACTOR, which is a creative hub. Definitely venture to Lekki Conservation Centre for picnic or to climb the popular canopy walkway. Also, go to Tarkwa Bay for the beach experience and lastly, find a good food pop-up.

"Wetin old woman siddon for ground see, pikin wey stand on top tree no go ever fit see am"

PIDGIN PROVERB

Lagos Island, known to residents as "Isale Eko", is the commercial headquarters of Lagos state. It is connected to the mainland by three bridges: Eko Bridge, Third Mainland Bridge, and Carter Bridge. It is linked to neighbouring island Victoria Island and Ikoyi. Many of the banks in Nigeria have their headquarters on Lagos Island. Lagos Island is also home to Balogun, the biggest open-air market in West Africa, where much of the commerce in Lagos happens.

LAGOS ISLAND

Balogun Market 🛍️

This market is one of the biggest open markets in Nigeria and West Africa. There is almost nothing that you cannot find in this market. Many come here to buy affordable fabrics as it is the hub for fabrics and textiles in the city. As one of the busiest markets in Nigeria, a visit can be overwhelming so try to go with local friends if possible and when the sun is at bay. Bring your negotiation game here, as you will need it to get a decent deal. A rule of thumb for shopping here: never pay the first price uttered by the vendor. Balogun Market is located on a stretch of *Balogun Street, off Broad Street, Lagos Island.*

Balogun Market

Freedom Park

Freedom Park 🌳 🍴 🎭 📚

Freedom Park is a former prison that has been turned into an enchanting public park. The prison was named Her Majesty's Broad Street Prison and it was later reconstructed to preserve the history and cultural heritage of the Nigerian people. Today the park serves as a national memorial, historical landmark, cultural site, and arts and recreation centre. The grounds provide a home for cultural events and it is home to the Wole Soyinka Art Gallery. Freedom Park has an array of shops and bars to get food and drinks from while you relax in the courtyard. It is also known for hosting many literary events like poetry gatherings and literary festivals. Freedom Park is located on *Broad Street, Lagos Island.*

Tafawa Balewa Square

Tafawa Balewa Square

Named after the first prime minister in Nigeria, Sir Abubakar Tafawa Balewa, the square holds a historical place in the history of Nigeria because it is where Nigeria celebrated its independence on October 1, 1960. Popularly called TBS, this historical monument was a former horse-racing track until 1972 when it was converted into the park. It is a wonderful place to take part in the art culture of Lagos. The first thing you notice at the entrance are the four mounted statues of horses and the seven red eagles over the gate of the square. It also serves as a ceremonial ground, spanning across 14.5 hectares. The square has hosted inaugurations of governors, major trade fairs, and large concerts. Tafawa Balewa Square is located at *45/57 Massey Bamgboshe Street, Lagos Island.*

Rele Gallery 🎭 🏛

Looking for a modern and contemporary art gallery that represents artists across Nigeria? Then Rele Gallery is the place to visit. The female-owned gallery strives to be innovative with its exhibitions, with the aim of challenging the way art is presented, consumed, and collected. The founder and owner, Adenrele Sonariwo, is an award-winning gallerist and curator. Take a guided tour and explore art like never before. Rele Gallery is located at *5 Military Street, Onikan, Lagos Island.*

Rele Gallery

The Muson Centre 🎭 🏛️

The Muson Centre is an amazing organisation that was founded in 1983 as a result of the interaction and commitment of several friends – Mr Akintola Williams, Mr Louis Mbanefo, Chief Ayo Rosiji, Chief Rasheed Gbadamosi, and Mrs Francesca Emanuel – who had immense love and appreciation for classical music. The main objective of the centre is to promote the understanding, enjoyment, and performance of classical and contemporary music in Nigeria. From musical theatre to concerts to stage plays, the Muson Centre hosts it all. Make sure to review the centre's programme to catch a show while in town. The Muson Centre is located at *8/9 Marina Road, Onikan, Lagos Island.*

The Muson Centre

Ghana High Restaurant

Ghana High Restaurant

Named because of its proximity to the old Ghana High Commission building, Ghana High is a Nigerian food spot that is very popular with locals because of its authentic taste and affordability. Their Jollof Rice, as well as their beans and plantain, have been raved to be one of the most authentic in Lagos. You can either choose to dine indoors or take out your meal to feast comfortably at home. Ghana High Restaurant is located at *34 Macarthy Street, Lagos Island.*

INTERVIEW *with*
AKAH NNANI

NOLLYWOOD ACTOR

Akah Nnani is a Nigerian-born actor, TV host, content creator, and YouTuber. The young and talented actor has been cast in several MNET Africa television films, web series, feature films, and he aspires to soon have a global brand. Akah Nnani is regarded as one of the most talented and natural media personalities in Nigeria. He has had the opportunity to interview a number of African music and film celebrities, while also being a guest on top TV and radio shows in the pan-African landscape.

Akah, like many Lagosians, left a life in the corporate industry in pursuit of a creative one in the Nollywood industry. The best in Nollywood, fashion recommendations, and tourist recommendations are some of what he exclusively shares with us.

What is your relationship with Lagos?

I was actually born in Imo state, which is located in south-eastern Nigeria. I worked in the telecommunications industry in Lagos before I then decided to pursue my Nollywood career. Lagos built my career.

In one sentence, how would you describe Lagos?

The land of opportunity. Yes, because everything happens here. The city is full of hustle, bustle, and competition. The competition is good because it pushes you to get better, do better, and fight for your dreams. You find that Lagosians are competing with global standards, constantly striving for the best.

Where in Lagos do you live and where is your favourite area in the city and why?

I live in Mobil estate near Ajah. Lekki is certainly my favourite area. Lekki has developed over the years and has become self-sufficient. You have access to many facilities including 24-hour supermarkets. Overall, things are much saner on the island (Victoria Island–Ikoyi–Lekki axis) than on the Lagos mainland. I used to live on the mainland before, but I was convinced to move to the island by some friends. I prefer it here.

What inspires you most about the city?

The truth is that the city can be hectic and draining at times. We are always striving for more because obligations keep rising. You can't afford to be broke in Lagos. Yes! That is what inspires me about this city. Lagos pushes you not to be lazy. You have to stay alert and be driven to succeed in the city. I am inspired by the many people who are pursuing excellence; those that are aspiring towards their best.

Tell us a bit about the industry that you have developed your career in: Nollywood?

The Nigerian movie industry, "Nollywood", is swiftly changing, from a period of only releasing home videos, we have come to cinema and now we are beginning to export content to the world. The industry is playing on the global stage now. With the release of *Black Panther*, studios are more than ever in need of African stories that the market has shown and proven it is ready to consume. Everyone is looking for that original African story. The likes of producers like Mo Abudu and Biola Alabi have shown they have what it takes to compete on the global stage. The Nollywood industry has a great future ahead of it.

What Nollywood movies would you recommend for those looking to get acquainted with Nigerian culture?

Ojukokoro is a really great movie (produced by Dare Olaitan). *Isoken* is also a great movie that does well to show the beauty of Nigeria and our culture (produced by Jadesola Osiberu). '76 is a very good movie that details the life of a Nigerian army officer during the coup and what he experienced. So yes, I have given you something relating to history, culture, and tales of the Nigerian hustle.

As an actor, you spend a lot of time on set, working on scripts, etc. Where do you go to escape the Lagos hustle?

A very amazing place – my bed. Because I am on set or being lodged at hotels because of my filming schedule, I am away from home a lot. So when I get a chance to return home to the comfort of my surroundings, I cherish it. My home is a place of rest and a chance to slip away from the world.

What is your favourite Nigerian dish?

Jollof rice is top on my list. Because I am currently on a healthy eating path, I plan to reduce my consumption of jollof rice. Fried plantain and eggs with a side of beans is also a strong contender. Or even bread and beans. As you can see, I love Nigerian food.

Where can tourists find local delicacies to try?

Jevinik is a great place to try. They will give you food and you will be angry at the portions they will serve to you. The portions are huge. The African section at Mega Chicken is also great. Try the starch and Banga Soup. The first time I had it and I was like, "God, is this what you have blessed me with?!" The food there will change your life. Habib Yoghurt is also a great place to try the Northern delicacy: try Fura De Nunu, which is a millet and aged milk blend. They have a location in Ikoyi, Surulere, and also just before Ajah.

What is the coolest place to be seen in Lagos?

There are many places to be seen. Cool kids hang out in Were House in Lekki. Hard Rock Café seems like the go-to place to vibe off on a Friday night. The beach by Hard Rock is also a lovely place to chill and go for a lovely stroll.

What does a typical Saturday look like in your life?

I wake up and head off to the gym. For lunch, I pop to Mega Chicken to grab some food as I don't cook. I then head off to set. If I don't have work, I go to the Lagos mainland to spend some quality time with bae, my girlfriend. Then I tend to meet up with friends for drinks after dinner. Yes, that is pretty much my day. Sometimes I MC at events but you won't normally find me at weddings like the typical Lagosian. A typical Saturday by a typical Lagosian will be spent at an Owanbe (party) or wedding.

Akah has since this interview married his girlfriend.

What is a typical day in the life of an actor in Lagos?

It's all go-go. Either I am on set in front of the camera, learning characters, or cooking up content as I am also a vlogger. I am constantly working on development ideas and content for brands I work with and also for myself. I self-produce much of the content you see on my YouTube channel.

What book would you recommend for those looking to learn more about Nigeria?

Half of the Yellow Sun by Chimamanda Ngozi Adichie and also There Was a Country by Chinua Achebe.

What would you change about Lagos?

Traffic! The traffic in Lagos can be mind-blowing. It is one of those kinds that can make a 15-minute journey seem like eternity. Yes, I wish we did more about reducing traffic.

For those with limited time in the city, what are the top five places you would recommend for a visit?

Number one has to be Nike Art Gallery to see the creativity of artists in Nigeria, then try suya (grilled meat) from Glover Court Suya in Ikoyi. Definitely, I would recommend Tarkwa Bay Beach, which is just a 20-minute ride from Victoria Island. Experiencing a local church service is also a must so they can experience how we pray. Finally, I would take them to West Africa's biggest open market, Balogun Market, where they can shop for inexpensive souvenirs or dashikis. I think these things will be a great representation of Lagos.

As an actor who has a taste for looking good, where do you go shopping for clothes?

Jeff Urban Clothing is a particular designer that I love. He is amazing at what he does. He made me an incredible outfit I wore to my fellow actor Zainab Balogun's wedding. Chavvy Clothing is also good. His signature outfit is African-inspired joggers and jumpers.

"Good name better pass gold and silver."

PIDGIN PROVERB

Ikeja is the capital of Lagos state. It is home to Lagos' two airports, namely the Murtala Mohammed International Airport and the MMA2 domestic terminal. Many of the state buildings are found in Ikeja, as well as the state secretariat, which is located in Alausa. Like Victoria Island, it also houses many large corporations, including some of the oldest multinational companies like Cadbury and Unilever. Ikeja also has its members-only Lagos Country Club and it also boasts many international hotels. High-brow neighbourhoods around Ikeja include Opebi, Ogba, Maryland, Government Residential Area (G.R.A.), Agidingbi, and Alausa. Ikeja is known for its nightlife, found in many bars and clubs as well as its vibrant commercial activity. One of the must-visit places is the New Africa Shrine by the late Fela Kuti. The popular Computer Village, which stands as one of the largest electronics and gadgets hub in Africa, is also found in Ikeja.

IKEJA

The New African Shrine 🍸 🏛 🎭

The host location for the annual Felabration Music Centre, the New African Shrine is a cultural entertainment hub. The New African Shrine was created as a legacy for Fela Anikulapo Kuti, a Nigerian icon, Afrobeats musician, and human-rights activist. Order a bottle of palm wine drink, watch the live band play, and enjoy the dancing from the many gracefully talented dancers. Nigerians from all walks of life and expats alike find themselves here. The Shrine also showcases photo galleries of Fela Anikulapo Kuti and sells a few African inspired merchandise. Try and go on Thursdays and Sundays to watch Femi Kuti or Seun Kuti, the sons of the late icon, perform live. On July 3, 2018, French President Emmanuel Macron visited the Shrine and pre-launched the Season of African Cultures 2020 in France. This is undoubtedly something you MUST DO during your visit to Lagos. The New African Shrine is located on *Nerdc Road, Agidingbi, Ikeja.*

The New African Shrine

Ikeja City Mall

Ikeja City Mall

Ikeja City Mall is one of the most frequented malls in Lagos and it is no surprise why. Located in the Alausa region of Ikeja, this modern shopping centre hosts more than 100 shops, a cinema, and many restaurants. Many local and international retailers have found their base here. The mall provides a diverse, comfortable, clean, safe, and convenient experience including shopping, entertainment, and leisure under one roof. Ikeja City Mall is located at *174/194 Obafemi Awolowo Way, Alausa, Ikeja.*

Radisson Blu Hotel Ikeja

Radisson Blu Hotel Ikeja

Just five kilometres from the Murtala Muhammed International Airport and a 20-minute drive from Ikeja City Mall, Radisson Blu Hotel Ikeja is a top choice for the business and leisure travellers who find themselves on the Lagos mainland. The hotel boasts 94 rooms, including 27 spacious suites, free high-speed wireless internet facilities, great cuisine, and more. The hotel is also home to state-of-the-art facilities to host business meetings and events. With a total meeting space of 2,047 square metres, the hotel can host 400 delegates, theatre style. The property is located at *38/40 Isaac John Street, Ikeja.*

Kalakuta Republic Museum

Take a tour of this museum, a former home to the legendary Afrobeats singer and human-rights activist Fela Anikulapo Kuti, and get a history lesson into Fela's life, his many wives, and his art. The museum features Fela's bedroom which has remained untouched since his death in 1997. The museum also hosts a newly formed hotel and a rooftop and bar with an enviable view of Ikeja. The museum is located at *7 Gbemisola Street, Ikeja.*

Kalakuta

INTERVIEW
with

ADENIKE OYETUNDE

ON-AIR & MEDIA PERSONALITY, DISABILITY ADVOCATE

One of the biggest on-air and media personalities in Nigeria, Adenike Oyetunde has carved a niche for herself in the industry. Adenike is a trained lawyer-turned-broadcaster with Nigeria Info FM and an author. Being a lawyer had always been her childhood dream and then she found a new passion for media. Today, she has changed lives through her work. She is also a TEDx speaker who spoke on philanthropy in the TEDxGbagada event in 2017.

Though her work focuses on radio, Adenike is also the founder of Amputees United, an organisation built to support amputees within and outside Nigeria. She is passionate about this organisation as she too had one of her limbs amputated at the age of 20. It has been 12 years since her surgery. Here, she gives us insights into why she loves Lagos and never wants to leave.

What are you currently working on?

I am working on developing my NGO Amputees United to help those with disabilities. My NGO Amputees United is very important to me. I advocate for persons living with disabilities because I'm a person living with disabilities in Lagos myself. I am also finishing up my book, which will be my life's story thus far.

How would you describe the typical Nigerian radio listener?

The typical Nigerian radio listener knows it all, wants to be heard, and always has something to say. Some people are either left or right wing. There is no middle ground. Highly opinionated. Some people have a problem with a woman telling them this is the way things are.

Have you always lived in Lagos?

Yes, I have always lived in Lagos. The only time I stepped out of Nigeria was for three months when I was in Houston, Texas, for a medical visit. But I also completed my undergraduate degree in Ogun state. I went to primary school in Ikoyi and Victoria Island, areas which I loved growing up in. I currently live in Ikoyi.

How would you describe your home area in Ikoyi?

Ikoyi is for the rich. Unfortunately, the middle class is slowly and gradually (and sadly) fading away. Somehow, I have been opportune to stay somewhere that my finances would not have allowed. I think in the course of life, meeting people and networking, I got the opportunity to be back where my childhood begun so. To me, it's like I'm back home. Would I stay here longer? I don't know. Do I want to? Yes, I want to because Ikoyi is home. Ikoyi is my favourite part of Lagos.

What do you like most and least about Lagos?

Least has to be traffic. Most is certainly the people and also the food and places to visit. The funny thing about traffic is you find yourself missing it when you step out of the city. I find the spirit of mine that is missing traffic! People, because there's such a diversity of people in Lagos, from the passionate to the energetic.

What do you like about places and food in Lagos?

For places, I have noticed so many new diverse establishments popping up. Just last night I was hanging with some friends at a new restaurant in Lekki. Food!! I am a foodie, I love to eat out, especially when it is not on my bill. My favourite place in Ikoyi is Samantha's Bistro. I love the open vibe. My favourite meal though is our Nigerian beans and plantain. I also love white rice and turkey stew.

What inspires you most about Lagos?

The spirit. There is always a party somewhere. There is always someone selling something to you that you already own, but selling it with such enthusiasm that you stand in awe that this hustle is real. THE SPIRIT of never giving up.

We heard that you love to read. What book would you recommend for those that have never been to Nigeria?

Yes, I recently developed my love for reading. I would recommend a book about Nigeria: Chinua Achebe's *There Was a Country*, Chimamanda Adichie's earlier work *Purple Hibiscus*. Chimamanda's imagination is amazing.

Where do you like to eat?

Sugarcane in Victoria Island. They always give you some cinnamon popcorn whilst you are waiting for you meal; it is delicious. I love to eat suya from Glover Court Suya in Ikoyi at least once a week.

Where would you take a tourist to eat authentic Nigerian food?

For Amala and Soup, Olaiya Amala in Surulere. For their amazing local fish, Utazi on Etim Inyang Crescent in Victoria Island. For Jollof Rice, we would go to Ghana High on Lagos. For Fish Pepper Soup, Farm City in Lekki is great. The Isi Ewu, Chicken Isi Ewu, and Ofada Rice at the restaurant in Freedom Park is great.

How do you spend a typical Friday or Saturday evening?

I love to hang out with friends so maybe we go to the movies. There are a number of cinemas here on the island. We even have an IMAX cinema in Lekki. Other times we go to dinner. I love to go to comedy skits and music shows. In particular, I have enjoyed music shows from Nigerian artists like Asa, Falz, and Adekunle Gold. They are worth checking out.

A business traveller in Lagos has only a weekend to spare to explore Lagos. Recommend five things they should do.

1. Visit Nike Art Gallery in Lekki
2. Go to Freedom Park (Lagos Island) or Bogobiri (Ikoyi) for an entertainment event (but check the schedule)

3. Have lunch at Olaiya Amala restaurant in Surulere
4. Visit the Lekki Conservation Centre and climb the canopy walkway
5. Visit a beach, either Ilashe beach or Tarkwa Bay

You mentioned your love of Nigerian music. Who are your favourite artists and why?

It would have to be Simi, Brymo, and Bantu. I love the style of music that they do, which is why SMOOTH FM radio station is my go-to radio station. They take you down memory lane. When you're done with those artists, you can then listen to the likes of DavidB and Nonso Bassey.

What do you love about your job as a broadcaster?

I love my job. My job makes a lot of people think I am intelligent. I love the fact that I have a platform that allows me to spark conversations. I remember we had a conversation about old people's homes with many people disagreeing with the notion, saying it is "un-African". We dived into the topic and talked about the negatives of leaving aged parents in the care of those that are not equipped to take care of them. I like those conversations where we can talk about things, be enlightened, and stop living in denial. Also the reach of my platform is humbling, when people tune in from London and New York for my show.

Do you think On-Air Personalities are still relevant in the world today?

Sure! Information dissemination is still vital anywhere in the world. Traditional media as we know it – newspapers, terrestrial TV – is changing. Radio still remains one of the biggest tools for dissemination of information to the public in Nigeria. But radio is also catching up and utilising new technologies. Many of our listeners can now join us on YouTube or on Instagram Live. On-Air-Personalities are now becoming personalities, brands in themselves, and their roles have extended to manage this new age media.

Adenike has since this interview authored her autobiography, *Adénìké.*

"Cassava today fit be Garri tomorrow."

PIDGIN PROVERB

Badagry, which is located at the far end of Lagos, is a historical town known for its ties to the slave trade. The town is bordered on the south by the Gulf of Guinea and surrounded by creeks, islands, and a lake. The town of Badagry was an important slave route in West Africa. In the early 1500s slaves were transported from West Africa to America through the town. Many were also transported to Europe, South America, and the Caribbean. Today, Badagry is a thriving community headed by chiefs. Badagry is a great place to go relax, get away from the hustle and bustle of Lagos, and to embrace history and culture. There are beaches, museums, and historical monuments in Badagry, making Badagry a prime and popular tourist destination. Some of the best places to visit when you're in Badagry include: the first storey building in Nigeria, the Badagry Coconut Beach, the Whispering Palms Resort, and the Agia Tree Monument, to mention a few. Many of the buildings have been preserved in their original form so that tourists can unearth the impact of this era.

BADAGRY

The First Storey Building in Nigeria

The First Storey Building in Nigeria

The First Storey Building was built by Rev. C. A. Gollmer as the C.M.S. vicarage headquarters. The foundation of the first storey building in Nigeria was laid in 1842 and completed in June of 1845. This ancient structure was occupied by Samuel Ajayi Crowther, the first African C.M.S. bishop. He is also known for translating the Holy Bible from English to Yoruba. The building was used as a vicarage for the Saint Thomas Anglican Church. Take a tour of the building with a guide to take you back in history. The First Storey Building is located on *Marina Road, Badagry.*

The Agai Tree Monument 🏛 ⏳ ⛪

The legendary Agai Tree lived for about 350 years and it was about 160 feet high and 30 feet in circumference. The tree stood at the heart of the town, beside the present Badagry Town Hall. Before the arrival of the Christian missionaries, the spot of the tree was a famous public square used for traditional, social, and religious functions. The gospel of Christianity was first preached in Nigeria under this tree by Reverend Thomas Birch Freeman of Wesleyan Mission, on September 24, 1842, and later by Reverend Henry Townsend of Church Missionary Society. While the tree fell as a result of a rainstorm in 1959, a cenotaph currently stands in its place. It is located on *Soglo Way, Badagry.*

The Agai Tree Monument

The Badagry Heritage Museum

The Badagry Heritage Museum is owned and managed by the Lagos State Ministry of Tourism and Intergovernmental Relations. The museum has the most comprehensive collection on the transatlantic slave trade in Nigeria and it consists of eight galleries: Introduction, Capture, Facilitators, Equipment, Resistance and Punishment, Industry, Integration, Abolition, and Badagry. The museum is open Monday to Saturday, from 9 a.m. to 5 p.m. It is located on *Lander Road, Badagry.*

The Badagry Heritage Museum

Brazilian Slave Barracoon

Brazilian Slave Barracoon

The Barracoon was the store where slaves were kept before the arrival of the slave ships. Located opposite the Slave Port, the structure, which was declared a national monument in 1940, is situated within the Seriki Abass Court. Chief Seriki Williams Abass was a slave turned slave merchant. He was bought by a Dutch owner "Mr Williams" and taken to Brazil where he became a member of domestic staff and learned to read and write in Dutch, English, Spanish and Portuguese. He later returned to Nigeria and became a slave business owner under the the guidance of his owner, Mr Williams. The tour of the museum will take you through the thought patterns of the slave owners, what currency they traded slaves in, and the conditions in which slaves were kept until they were sold. The Brazilian Slave Barracoon is located on *Marina Road, Badagry.*

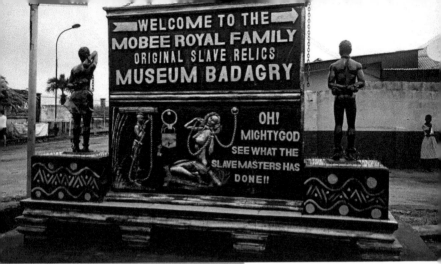

Chief Mobee Family Slaves Relics Museum

Chief Mobee Family Slaves Relics Museum

Located at the Mobee Family Compound in the Boekoh Quarters of Badagry, this one-room museum contains the relics used during the slave trade between the 16th and 19th centuries. Some of the exhibits range from leg and neck chains to ankle shackles and mouth clips. The Mobee family were able to assemble the relics due to their acknowledgement of the roles of their ancestors in the slave trade and its abolition. The tour guides on-site give deep insights into the horrific story of the slave trade. Chief Mobee Family Slaves Relic Museum is located on *Mobee Street, Badagry.*

Slave Route: Point Of No Return

This is the path where the slaves were driven through, between the 16th and 19th centuries. It is about a 20-minute walk from the Gberefu Jetty to the seashore called "Point of No Return", where slaves boarded ships to unknown destinations. The slaves were forced to drink from a sacred well known as the Slave Spirit Attenuation Well, which still stands today. The well was believed to make them less aggressive and to make them lose their memories. It is located at Gberefu Sea Beach across the Lagoon, directly opposite the *Slave Port Badagry on Marina Road.*

Slave Route: Point Of No Return

Badagry Slave Port ⏳ 🏛️ 🏰

Badagry Slave Port was opened in the 16th century and by the beginning of the 18th century it had become the biggest port in West Africa where slaves were loaded into boats for onward shipment to Europe and the Americas. The port is now being regenerated into an ultra-modern garden and recreational centre, with the original spots being preserved for tourists. Badagry Slave Port is located on *Marina Road, Badagry.*

Badagry Slave Port

Whispering Palms Resort

Whispering Palms Resort

Explore the idyllic town of Iworo/Ajido off the Badagry expressway by visiting the most notable resort in Badagry. Whispering Palms Resort is a great option if you are planning an overnight trip in Badagry, as the road to Badagry can be long and bumpy. The resort is popular on weekends as it is one of the few establishments in the area. Bask in the serenity of the greenery of this down-to-earth resort. Many activities are available, from water sports to a games arena. Bring your own picnic here or eat from the restaurants, but don't forget to order a fresh cold coconut from the coconut bar at the resort. Whispering Palms Resort is located in *Adijo Town, Badagry.*

Vlekete Slave Market

Vlekete Slave Market

Vlekete Market is one of the oldest markets in West Africa. It was opened in 1502 and is located in the heart of the town, at Posukoh Quarters of Badagry. Millions of Africans were sold from this market as slaves and shipped to European and American countries. It was recorded that a cannon was used in exchange for 100 slaves, as well as a dry gin in exchange for two able-bodied men. When different slave merchants auctioned slaves, all slaves were marched down to their various cells in different parts of Badagry, typically along the coast, where they remained for three months under terrible conditions, chained from head to toe. Vlekete Market is now an evening market and a tourist centre. It is located on *Market Road, Badagry.*

The First Primary School in Nigeria

The First Primary School in Nigeria was established in 1845, within the First Storey Building premises, and it was called Nursery of the Infant Church. Today, the school has been moved from the old vicarage to its permanent site at Posukoh Quarters, and its name changed to St. Thomas' Anglican Nursery and Primary School. The school is still functional, and the relic of the old building can still be seen today. The school is located on *Market Road, Badagry.*

The First Primary School in Nigeria

Suntan Beach 🏝️ 🌳

Suntan Beach is a government-owned public beach located west of Lagos city. The beach is located about a 15-minute car ride from the border of Benin Republic and is very popular with locals of Badagry as well as residents of Benin Republic. There are many activities, from horseback riding to swimming. Beach cabanas can also be rented for a fee. The beach gets very busy during public holidays. It is located off *Lagos-Badagry Expressway.*

Suntan Beach

"No be everythin wey touch your hand you go put for mouth."

PIDGIN PROVERB

If you're looking for a central entertainment hub on Lagos mainland, then Surulere is an amazing area. It is a mid-point that conveniently connects the city's mainland with the island, making its highly residential system a haven for those who work on the island and live on the mainland. With an amazing blend of upscale bars and clubs, shopping malls, as well as a variety of restaurants, it is easy to get comfortable in Surulere. Its affordability, when compared to areas like Victoria Island, Lekki, and Ikoyi, also make it a top choice. One thing the area is known for is its street foods, best had from local food kiosks known as "Bukas". From Suya to Shawarma you get to take your taste buds on a journey as you discover the exotic taste of Lagos.

SURULERE

Lounge 38 🍴 🍸

Lounge 38 is set on a popular street in Surulere and is home to a fast-food restaurant, bar, and club. The bar and club are popular with Lebanese and Indian expats and also with locals. The bar and club are open every day, with a variety of events organised in the evenings such as karaoke nights and ladies nights. Visit on Friday or Saturday if you want a nightclub vibe. Lounge 38 is located at *67 Bode Thomas Street, Surulere.*

Lounge 38

Olaiya Amala

Olaiya Amala

As its name reveals, Olaiya Amala is notably known for its Amala (a food made from yam or cassava flour). In the past, the restaurant was a no-frills Buka but has now evolved into a small, air-conditioned restaurant. This is a fast-food joint where only authentic Nigerian meals are served. The restaurant is very affordable (with a focus on the food not the service). You will find Nigerians from all walks of life and all backgrounds here. Olaiya Amala is located at *109 Akerele Street, Surulere.*

Suya Spot

Suya Spot 🍴

Suya Spot is a popular food joint in Surulere. Another place where both the elite and the working class can be found, Suya Spot's menu consists of Suya made from meats including beef, kidney, gizzard, liver, and shaki (tripe). If you're looking for a street snack to give you a tasty beef experience without breaking the bank, this place is a perfect choice. Suya Spot is located at *56 Akerele Street, Surulere*.

National Theatre

One of Lagos' biggest tourist attractions, National Theatre is the primary centre for performing arts in Nigeria and it hosts the collection of the National Gallery of Modern Nigerian Art. It was designed and constructed by Bulgarian construction companies and it resembles the Palace of Culture and Sports in Varna, Bulgaria. Located in the district of Igamu, it was completed in 1976 for the Festival of Arts and Culture (FESTAC) in 1977. Built during the military regime of Olusegun Obasanjo, the National Arts Theatres exterior is shaped like a military hat. The beautiful greenery surrounding the theatre make it popular with families who hold picnics there and those who want to experience arts and culture through theatre. National Theatre is located on *Iganmu Road, Surulere.*

National Theatre

MADE IN NIGERIA

BOOKS SET IN LAGOS/NIGERIA

Things Fall Apart by Chinua Achebe, 1958

Achebe's book *Things Fall Apart* chronicles pre-colonial life in the south-eastern part of Nigeria and the arrival of the Europeans during the late 19th century. Achebe's account of life in pre-colonial Nigeria is told from the point of view of his protagonist, Okonkwo, while using Okonkwo's daily travails to reveal a broader societal system. It guides us through the intricacies of Igbo culture and takes its scenes from the life of Nigeria's Igbo society vividly. *Things Fall Apart* became one of the most important books in African literature, selling more than 20 million copies around the world. It has been translated into 57 languages, making Achebe the most translated African writer of all time.

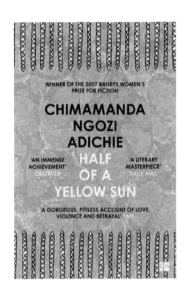

Half of a Yellow Sun by Chimamanda Ngozi Adichie, 2006

Epic, ambitious, and wonderfully written, *Half of a Yellow Sun* is a remarkable novel about moral responsibility, the end of colonialism, ethnic allegiances, class and race – and about the ways in which love can complicate them all. Chimamanda Ngozi Adichie has been referred as, "the 21st-century daughter of Chinua Achebe", by the *Washington Post*'s Book World. The book has been made into a movie and has won multiple awards across the globe.

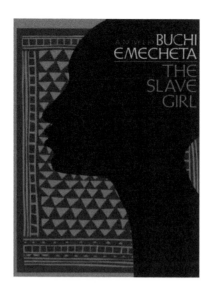

The Slave Girl by Buchi Emecheta, 1977

Buchi Emecheta's books are themed around child slavery, motherhood, female independence, and freedom through education. This book tells the story of "twice-born" Ogbanje Ojebeta, mythical traditional ideologies that border on rebirth and reincarnation. The protagonist, following the death of her parents, is betrayed by her older brother and sold into domestic slavery. *The Slave Girl* won the Jock Campbell Award from the *New Statesman* in 1978. The novel was Emecheta's fourth book out of more than 20 that she has written. She has been characterised as the first successful black woman novelist living in Britain after 1948.

MOVIES

The Wedding Party 2: Destination Dubai
by Niyi Akinmolayan, 2017

As of 2018, *The Wedding Party 2: Destination Dubai* was the highest grossing Nigerian film of all time. This 2017 Nigerian romantic comedy drama was directed by Niyi Akinmolayan and is a sequel to *The Wedding Party*, which won the hearts of many across the world. The film showcases the colourful, chaotic and memorable journey of the joining of a Nigerian family and an upper-class British family. *The Wedding Party* was acquired by Netflix and is available worldwide.

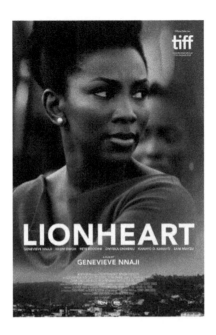

Lionheart by Genevieve Nnaji, 2018

One of Nigeria's iconic actresses and producers, Genevieve Nnaji made her directorial debut with *Lionheart*. The film deals with the everyday sexism that saturates workplaces everywhere, and captures the delicate balance between honouring one's family while finding the courage to strike out on one's own. The worldwide rights for *Lionheart* were acquired by Netflix, which was announced at the eve of its world premiere at the 2018 Toronto Film Festival.

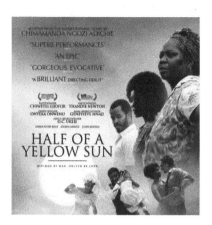

Half of a Yellow Sun by Biyi Bandele, 2013

This movie is a drama based on the novel of the same name by Chimamanda Ngozi Adichie. *Half of a Yellow Sun* is a love story that follows two sisters who are caught up in the outbreak of the Nigerian Civil War. The film premiered in the Special Presentation section at the 2013 Toronto International Film Festival. Biyi Bandele has also directed acclaimed films like *Fifty*, a Nigerian romantic-drama film. *Fifty* was also acquired by Netflix.

MUSIC REVEALING
OUR CULTURE

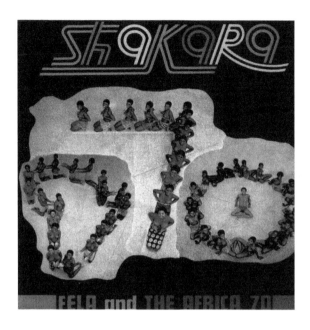

Shakara by Fela Anikulapo Kuti, 1972

Fela Anikulapo Kuti, whose birth name is Olufela Olusegun Oludotun Ransome-Kuti, was a Nigerian legend who thrived as a multi-instrumentalist, musician, composer, human-rights activist, and pioneer of the Afrobeat music genre. *Shakara* consists of two 13-minute performances by Kuti's Africa 70 band: "Lady" and "Shakara (Oloie)". In "Lady", Kuti criticises the modern African women in a humorous way for becoming what he sees as overly westernised and embracing a Western view of feminism.

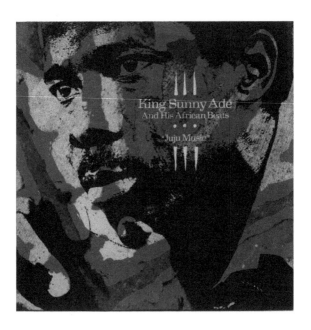

Juju Music by King Sunny Adé, 1982

Chief Sunday Adeniyi Adegeye MFR, who is known as King Sunny Adé, is a Nigerian singer-songwriter and multi-instrumentalist, who is known to have made the West African musical style of *jùjú* popular. *Juju Music* was the first worldwide release for King Sunny Adé. It was the major label debut of Nigerian *jùjú* band King Sunny Adé and his African beat. This Nigerian singer-songwriter and multi-instrumentalist in the West African musical style of *jùjú* was already established in Nigeria (where he was considered *jùjú* music's reigning monarch). The album was a commercial success, achieving #111 on Billboard's Pop Albums chart.

Beautiful Imperfection by Asa, 2010

The story of Asa, pronounced Asha, starts in Lagos, Nigeria. Asa is a Nigerian–French singer, songwriter, and recording artist. She has proven herself over the years as a musician with a unique style that is usually characterised by the depth of her lyrics. She released her second album, *Beautiful Imperfection*, on October 25, 2010. The album went platinum in 2011. The lead single from the album is called "Be My Man" and was released in late September 2010.

INDIGENOUS FASHION

CLAN

CLAN is a premium Ready-to-Wear brand which specializes in the needle-crafting of minimalist and distinct cosmopolitan pieces through the use of authentic techniques. With its first international showcase at the Mercedes Benz New York Fashion Week in 2014, CLAN has since gained international acclaim and traction for the superior quality and minimalist aesthetic of its clothing. Offering a range of pieces from work- wear to everyday basics to occasional wear, CLAN is quintessentially African in conceptualization while catering for the urban, social and corporate needs of the modern-day woman. Visit Clanrtw.com to find out more or go to *292F Ajose Adeogun Street, Victoria Island Lagos* for the CLAN experience.

ATAFO

One of the most influential African fashion designers, Mai Atafo created the formidable Atafo (formerly known as Mai Atafo) as an outlet to express himself. He is a Nigerian bespoke tailor and fashion designer who in 2011 added bridal his endeavours creating a world-renowned wedding line. His artistic and fashionable designs quickly caught the attention of the international fashion industry and has maintained his brand of quality ever since. ATAFO has been recognised around Africa for his contributions to fashion design and style. Visit atafo.africa to learn more about this brand.

Orange Culture

Adebayo Oke-Lawal launched his own line, Orange Culture, in 2011. In 2014, Orange Culture was a finalist for the LVMH Prize. Orange Culture brings a fresh, ultra-modern, savvy style to the street fashion space. As the brand evolves, Oke-Lawal continues to create androgynous looks that are defined by a mixture of Nigerian-inspired prints and contemporary urban streetwear. To date, Orange Culture has collaborated with international brands and recently, Oke-Lawal partnered with Nigerian artist Davido to design a limited-edition collection that was sold exclusively at Selfridges. Orange Culture's creation was driven by the need to create a brand that represented a sphere of men that are vulnerable, that are a bit soft; a man that's emotional. Visit orangeculture.com. ng to learn more about the brand.

Funke Ogunkoya-Futi is a Nigerian-British Media & Travel professional based between Lagos, Nigeria and London, United Kingdom. She worked in finance for six years in the UK and New York at a leading US investment bank before assuming a leadership role in one of Africa's largest and fastest-growing internet companies. She holds a BSc in Business Management from King's College London and an MBA from INSEAD Business School.

She was born in Osogbo, Nigeria and has visited over 40 countries to date. Funke Ogunkoya-Futi lives in Lagos with her daughter and husband, a Congolese-Canadian, who has come to see Lagos as a home away from home.

ABOUT THE
AUTHOR

Writing a travel guide is harder than I thought and more rewarding than I could have ever imagined. I have to start by thanking my husband Guy Futi for being my champion and driver to creating this piece of work, giving me the idea whilst we were in a bookshop in Boston, Massachusetts. Here, we both noticed the lack of representation of Nigerian travel guides in the travel section and decided I had to change that.

I am eternally grateful to my parents Anthony and Busayo Ogunkoya for their unwavering support in everything I do. Thank you for reviewing many drafts of this guide and championing me on. Your support gives me wings to fly. To my brother Folabi Ogunkoya, thank you for your unwavering guidance and support in all my endeavours.

A very special thanks to Mr Sola Oyinlola for providing an objective and thoughtful foreword for this travel guide.

To Chief Nike Davies-Okundaye, thank you for welcoming me into your gallery and treating me like a daughter, with such warmth and grace throughout our interactions and interview sessions.

To my interviewees: Akah Nnani, Alex Oke, Adenike Oyetunde and Samuel Ogundare, Thank you for sharing your unique and vivid perspectives of Lagos with me and the world. I am eternally grateful.

And to my photographer Don Dizzy of Dizzyframes LTD, thank you for your creativity and dedication as we set across Lagos State over three intense weeks to capture stunning images that truly depicts the magic that is Lagos.

ACKNOWLEDGEMENTS